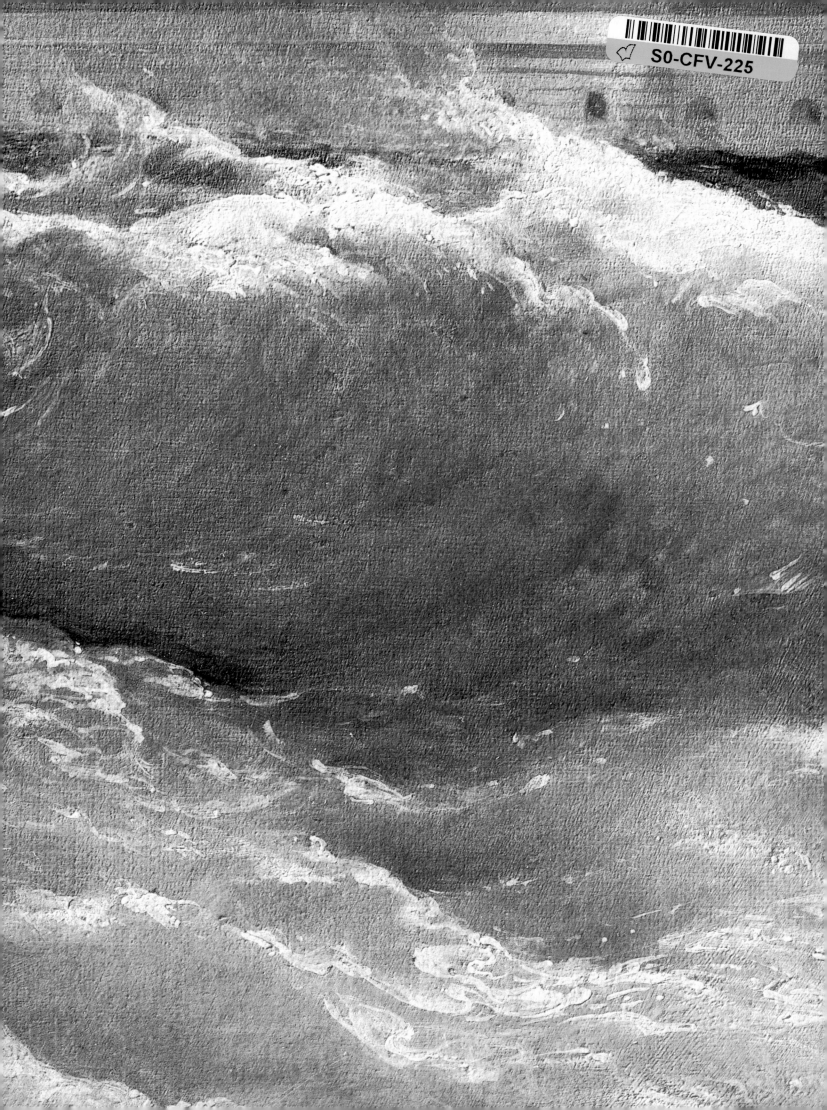

Newport News, Virginia

Guide to The

MARINERS'

Museum

Foreword

Archer Huntington, scholar and philanthropist, founded The Mariners' Museum in 1930 on the principle that it be *"devoted to the culture of the sea and its tributaries ... its conquest by man and its influence on civilization."* A further guiding principle is the concept of sea power as defined by the legendary naval historian Admiral Alfred Thayer Mahan in *The Influence of Sea Power Upon History 1660-1783*, published in 1890.

He described sea power as all the commercial, military, economic, political, artistic, scientific, and social elements that make up the fabric of a nation's maritime affairs and, ultimately, its national strength. It is within this overarching theme that The Mariners' Museum's time capsules and shards of history tell their stories.

The Mariners' Museum's collection of maritime artifacts, paintings, models, books, and photographs is one of the most comprehensive collections in any maritime museum in the Western Hemisphere. Throughout the Museum, the timeless story of man's reliance on the sea and fascination with its power to sustain, to delight, to destroy are revealed in all of its galleries, in each of its objects.

The collections of ninety figureheads, 1,450 ship models, and more than 700 navigational instruments rank among the finest in the western world. The photographic archives include 246,000 historical photographic prints and 350,000 negatives on a seemingly endless array of maritime subjects. More than 11,000 paintings, prints, drawings, engravings, and watercolors include works by James and John Bard, Robert Salmon, James Buttersworth, Antonio Jacobsen, Fitz Hugh Lane, Thomas Luny, Montague Dawson, and E.W. Cook. The ship models include builders' and boardroom models, World War II recognition training models, a silver and gold music box model, and the exquisite August F. Crabtree Collection of Miniature Ships, each constructed in exactly the same manner as its full-size counterpart.

No single aspect of The Mariners' Museum collections reflects its international character better than its collection of small craft from around the world. This collection includes a sampan, a gondola, a nineteenth-century lifesaving boat, a Brazilian jangada, classic mahogany yachts, two Herreshoff sloops, African canoes, and a Native American dugout canoe, circa 1630.

The Mariners' Museum Library is an international treasure with 75,000 specialized volumes and extensive archival material including ships' plans, maps and charts, ships' logs, and maritime account books. The library is also home to the Chris-Craft company archives and complete sets of *Harper's Weekly*, *Lloyd's Registry*, and the *Naval Chronicle*.

Although impressive by any standard, a numerical recitation of the Museum's holdings fails to convey its true dimensions and ultimate value. It does not capture the less exact, more significant measure of quality. And ultimately, it is the quality and depth of The Mariners' Museum which draw visitors, scholars, and museum professionals from all corners of the globe. This guide explores The Mariners' Museum's major themes, examines some of the more compelling items in its extensive collections, and offers a brief history of the founding of what has become one of the world's premier maritime museums.

JOHN B. HIGHTOWER
PRESIDENT AND CEO
THE MARINERS' MUSEUM

© 1997 BY THE MARINERS' MUSEUM,
NEWPORT NEWS, VIRGINIA.
ALL RIGHTS RESERVED.
MARINERS' MUSEUM PUBLICATION
NO. 46

PRINTED AND BOUND IN HONG KONG THROUGH
EMPOWERING PARTNERS, INC. USA

DESIGNED BY MATT HAHN, THINKDESIGN

PHOTOGRAPHY AND PROJECT MANAGEMENT BY
THE MARINERS' MUSEUM

ISBN 0-917376-47-1

Contents

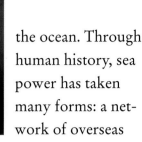

When Archer M. Huntington established The Mariners' Museum in 1930, he broke company with many other new American maritime museums by taking a decidedly global view of the sea and its effects on human history. In charging the institution with exploring "the culture of the sea," he began a process that would set The Mariners' Museum on a unique course for decades to come.

It is uncertain whether Huntington, son of railroad magnate and shipbuilder Collis P. Huntington, foresaw the leading international role that America would soon play. What is certain is that his global perspective has helped the Museum interpret this nation's position of influence over the waters of the world and upon the many shores beyond.

The rich collections developed over the decades are the perfect starting point for exploring the key concept of sea power—the use and control of the great rolling highway that is the ocean. Through human history, sea power has taken many forms: a network of overseas colonies, linked to the home country by a merchant marine; naval forces protecting colonial holdings, opening new areas to commerce and, most importantly, protecting the ships that make trade and communication possible; a thriving fishery tapping the living riches of the waters; and, more recently, the harvesting of undersea mineral resources.

In artifact, image, and written word, The Mariners' Museum illustrates the importance of sea power to the world and to America in particular. Exhibitions, specialized publications, and films work together to fulfill the Museum's educational mission.

Ongoing conservation programs aim to preserve crucial physical evidence of our maritime heritage. And as the Museum moves into the next century, it is using the new communication technology to forge global links as important as the busiest ocean trade routes.

Age of Exploration

The term "Age of Exploration" suggests a fixed time span, yet the work of exploration is ongoing, its roots traceable through thousands of years. Phoenicians, Egyptians, Greeks, Romans, and others probed the Mediterranean long before western Europeans launched concerted campaigns of exploration and expansion. Arabs, Asians, and Pacific islanders, too, accomplished impressive regional voyages of discovery at an early date. And beginning in the eighth century, Norse raiders ventured south and west, reaching Newfoundland in 1001.

Renaissance Europe looked both east and west in search of new sources of wealth. In the long run it was the development of New World resources like sugar cane, tobacco, wood, and fish, not gold, that provided the Old World with a dependable return on investment.

Expeditions sailed from Spain, Portugal, France, Britain, and Holland in search of political and economic opportunity, aided by new or improved navigational devices and increasingly sophisticated charts. The world we live in today is in large part the result of these European seaborne efforts.

In the early twentieth century, explorers turned their attention to unravelling the secrets of the icebound poles. More recent refinements to the science of navigation have included satellite systems and underwater technology, all aimed at aiding the new seaborne voyagers in this continuing "Age of Exploration."

Noua zemla

Noruegia

Suedia — Bergen — Solof ki — Pinego — Ysbug — Wilki — Obea — Calami

S. Nicolas — Nougroa — TARTARIA. — Grustina

Russia — Moskow — Volga R. — Bulgar — Marmorea — A

EVROPA — Cracow — Vissegroa — Astou — Don fl. — Cogia — Citraca — Rouore — Pagant

...mania. — Ausburch — Wien — Buda — Danub. fl. — Derbent — Mar de Bachu

Paris — Gallia — Lion — Italia — Raguza — Constantinopoli — Grecia — Goia — Canger — Trebizonda — Bazru — Armenia. — Mar de Bachu

Natolia. — Alepo — Halla — Mosul — Persia.

Hispania — Corsica — Sicilia — Iudia — Ciprus — Soria. — Baldach — Saura — Re

Lisbon — Scandia — Septa — Alger — Bugia — Tunis — Hierusalem — Siras — M

Barba — ria. — Tripoli — Luncho — Angela — Alexandria — Cairo — Medina — Congas

Marocco — Berdoa — Aegyptus

Auzichi

Alhamara — Hair — Targa — Digir — Albaidi — Geogra — Mecha — Quixibi — Cal

Argin — AFRICA. — Cano — Borno — Nubia — Arabia.

Hoden — Agi — Suachem — Zibet — Fartach

Darm — symba. — Guanguara — Nubia — Lacuri — Aden

Tombotu — Melli — Zigide — Vella

Cago — Mellegete — Mina — Benin — Ambia — Chax umo — Zelia — Zacot

Serra liona — Biafar — Nilus fl. — Asuga — Magadaxo

C. da Verga — R. Dangala — Abissi — ni. — Braua

C. de 3 puntas — Principe — Gaga

S. Tomas — Manicon- go. — Melinde — Vasco de Acuna

Croce le — S. Matheo — Nobon — Maceria. — Caigra — Mel inde — Adarno

Ascension — Vamba — Mani con go. — Dangara — Quiloa

OCEANVS AE- THIOPICVS — C. f. — Cotta — Leuma — Mozam bique — Liona

S. Helena — C. de aveis — i. Gebage — Inf. S. Laurenty — S. Apollonia

C. Neg. — Zimbro — Degme

Mas de ainidaes — G. de las bueltas — G. de S. Antonio — Buro — Mascar — Bay

Tristan de Acuna — Cayneca — Coreada — Punta de S. Maria — C. folido — Iuan de Lisboa

C. Bone Sper — C. de las uacas — Los Romeros

RIGHT
CARTOGRAPHER'S TOOLS,
EIGHTEENTH CENTURY
Various makers
By the eighteenth century,
cartographers were relying
on precision tools like these,
rather than imagination and
hand sketching, to produce
accurate maps and charts.

ABOVE
*GERARDUS MERCATOR AND
JODOCUS HONDIUS*,
SEVENTEENTH CENTURY
Unknown artist
Engraving, 18" x 20 ½"
Flemish cartographer
Gerardus Mercator is best
known for his "Mercator
projection" maps which,
though introduced in 1569,
did not come into widespread
use until the mid-1600s. The
mapmaker Jodocus Hondius
published an improved version
of his countryman's *Atlas*.

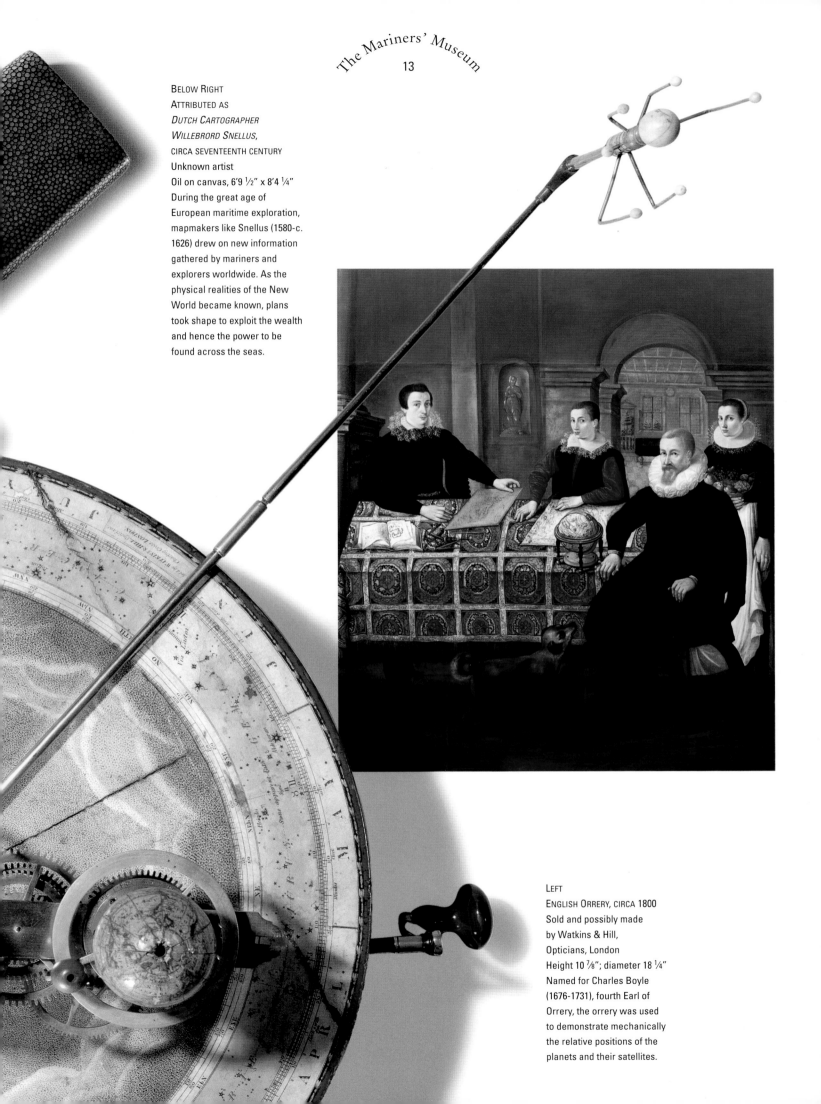

BELOW RIGHT
ATTRIBUTED AS
DUTCH CARTOGRAPHER
WILLEBRORD SNELLUS,
CIRCA SEVENTEENTH CENTURY
Unknown artist
Oil on canvas, 6'9 ½" x 8'4 ¼"
During the great age of
European maritime exploration,
mapmakers like Snellus (1580-c.
1626) drew on new information
gathered by mariners and
explorers worldwide. As the
physical realities of the New
World became known, plans
took shape to exploit the wealth
and hence the power to be
found across the seas.

LEFT
ENGLISH ORRERY, CIRCA 1800
Sold and possibly made
by Watkins & Hill,
Opticians, London
Height 10 ⅞"; diameter 18 ¼"
Named for Charles Boyle
(1676-1731), fourth Earl of
Orrery, the orrery was used
to demonstrate mechanically
the relative positions of the
planets and their satellites.

MODEL OF AN ARAB DHOW,
1993
William F. Wiseman,
modelmaker
Scale ⅜"=1'; length 37 ¾"
Arabs used these well-built
ships, called *bhums* or dhows,
for ocean voyages. Europeans
adapted the vessel's lateen
sail for their caravels and
nãos, but not its hull, which
was sewn together with
coconut rope. The figure
shown is using a *kamal*, an
ancient Arab instrument for
determining latitude.

LEFT
MODEL OF SIXTEENTH-CENTURY
SPANISH GALLEON, 1991
Kenneth Britten, modelmaker
Scale 1:48; length 41 ½"
The European carrack, popular as a merchant vessel in
the sixteenth century, was
superseded by the galleon,
which proved more stable
and could sail closer to
the wind. The well-armed
Spanish galleon was widely
copied by England and
other naval powers.

BELOW
MUSKET AND BAYONET,
CIRCA 1850
BOARDING PIKE
BOARDING AXE
These weapons proved espe-
cially useful in close combat
as sailors boarded enemy
ships. The axe was used to
disable a ship by cutting her
rigging and slashing her sails.
Boarding pike gift of Miss
Marjorie Borton

LEFT AND OPPOSITE PAGE (DETAIL)
PTOLEMAIC ARMILLARY SPHERE,
LATE EIGHTEENTH/
EARLY NINETEENTH CENTURY
Charles François Delamarche,
maker
Height 18 ½"
The armillary sphere, a skeletal
model of the celestial sphere,
was designed to give the mariner
knowledge of the arrangement
and motions of the heavenly
bodies. This late example reflects
the Ptolemaic-Christian tradition.

RIGHT
PTOLEMAIC ARMILLARY
SPHERE, 1747
Paul Sebastian Arrighi, maker
Height 14 ½"; diameter 9 ½"
Navigators found the
armillary sphere a helpful
three-dimensional repre-
sentation of the relationships
between Earth and the
heavens. Developed during
the Renaissance, the device
remained popular into the
nineteenth century.

LEFT
CHRONOMETER, CIRCA 1785
Josiah Emery
(Swiss, 1725-1796),
London, maker
10" x 6 ¼"
After John Harrison solved
the longitude riddle with his
"timekeeper" (chronometer),
Emery produced several
variations of the device,
experimenting with both the
design and the metal alloys.
This is one of only two exam-
ples of the Emery chro-
nometer known to exist.

RIGHT
BUTTERFIELD TYPE POCKET
SUNDIAL WITH COMPASS,
CIRCA 1680
J. Menard, Paris, maker
2 ¾" x 2 ⅛"
This type of sundial was
popular with the aristocracy
in the seventeenth century.
By aligning the style with
the Earth's axis and the
celestial pole, the user could
accurately determine the
time of day.

RIGHT
SAND GLASS, 1609
PROBABLY FRENCH
Height 4 ¾"
Sand glasses were used as
shipboard timepieces as early
as the fourteenth century. In
addition, a ship's speed could be
estimated by timing the paying
out of the chip log with a sand
glass like this.

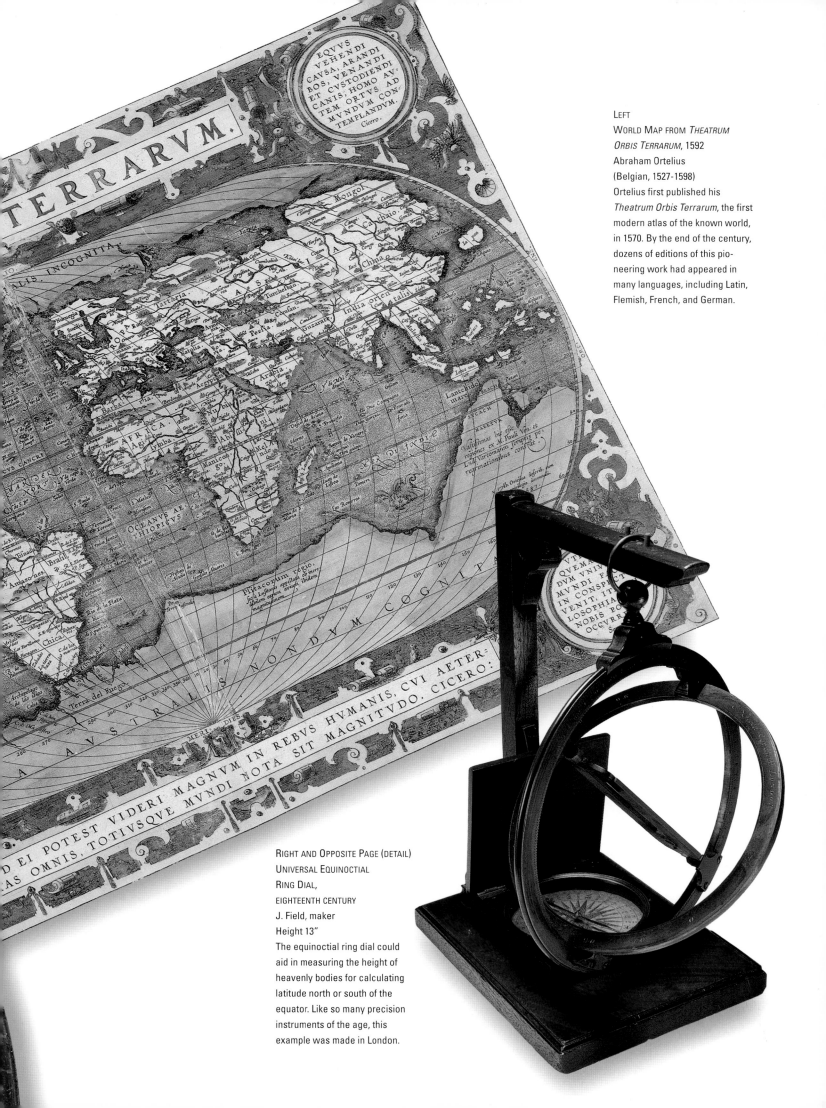

ABOVE
A JOURNAL OF A VOYAGE TO THE SOUTH SEAS, 1784
Sydney Parkinson (1745-1771)
Parkinson's lively journal, transcribed in this book, recounts HMS *Endeavour's* 1768-1771 voyage around the world under the command of Captain James Cook. The book includes vocabularies for Pacific island languages and various charts, including this one of the Bering Strait.

RIGHT
VUE DE L'ÎLE HUAHEIM DANS LA MER DU SUD ..., CIRCA 1777
James Cleveley
(English, b. 1750)
Wash drawing, 22" x 27 ¼"
Among the crewmen aboard Captain James Cook's flagship HMS *Resolution* in Huahine (Tahiti) was the carpenter James Cleveley, whose sketches were later worked up in watercolors by his brother John and illustrated in Cook's published works.

LEFT
PORTRAIT OF CAPTAIN
JAMES COOK, FROM *A
JOURNAL OF A VOYAGE TO
THE SOUTH SEAS*, 1784
Captain James Cook
(1728-1779) rose from humble
Yorkshire beginnings to be-
come one of Britain's best-
known seamen and explorers.
Charged by the British Ad-
miralty with searching for the
elusive "Terra Australis
Incognita" and recording
astronomical observations
en route, Cook made three
voyages of discovery, visiting
such far-flung places as
Tasmania, Batavia (now
Jakarta), and Easter Island.

BELOW
*A VOYAGE TO THE MALOUINE (OR
FALKLAND) ISLANDS*, 1773
Antoine Joseph Pernety
(1716-1801)
Translated from the French,
this book recounts a 1763-
1764 voyage to the Falkland
Islands under the command of
Comte Louis Antoine de
Bougainville, who tried to
establish a settlement there,
and two later voyages to the
Straits of Magellan.

Art of the Sea

RIGHT
MOCHE CEREMONIAL
STIRRUP SPOUT VESSEL,
CIRCA FIFTH CENTURY
Unknown maker
Height 9 ½"
The Moche of Northern
Peru were skilled artisans
in both metal and clay.
This ceramic vessel, with
its depiction of a dignitary
being towed across a river
on a raft, was used to pre-
serve ceremonial beer
from evaporation.

Over the centuries, the pervasive influence of the sea has been expressed by countless artists, writers, and composers in works both evocative and documentary.

Though Dutch "sea pieces" of the sixteenth and seventeenth centuries marked the beginning of a true marine painting tradition, it was the painters of the nineteenth century who raised marine art to new levels. The romantic movement found in the sea a favorite image, as did the "luminists" of mid-century, who sought to express the ideal of harmony between man and the natural world. Impressionism, with its interplay of light and reflection, helped carry marine art into the twentieth century.

The ship portrait, an ancient form, evolved as a distinct genre among the expansionist powers of seventeenth-century Europe. Eighteenth-century merchant shipowners used the ship portrait as an expression of pride in the source of their new-found prosperity. Until replaced by the photographer in the late nineteenth century, the ship portraitist remained the primary recorder of the vessels, trade, and maritime events of the time.

Not only in paint, but in ceramics, wood, marine ivory, bone, and even shells, artists have crafted objects grounded in the maritime world. Some forms of folk art such as scrimshaw, logbook sketches, and even tattoos, offer a glimpse of seafaring life over the centuries. Among the art forms most closely associated with the sea is model making. From the utilitarian shipbuilder's model to the most detailed masterpiece by a skilled artist, these miniature vessels can transport us to a different time and place.

BELOW AND RIGHT (DETAIL)
LIVERPOOL JUG,
OROZIMBO, OF BALTIMORE,
CIRCA 1806-1810
Herculaneum Pottery, maker
Height 11 ⅜"
Liverpool potters created
creamware jugs for the
owners and masters
of many American vessels.
This splendid example
commemorates the
Baltimore ship *Orozimbo*,
built in Mathews County,
Virginia, in 1805-1806.

SACRED

ABOVE
TURKISH SNUFF BOX,
NINETEENTH CENTURY
Silver
Diameter 2 ⅝"
SNUFF BOX, 1850
Parchment with gold rim
Diameter 2 ⅞"
The maritime world has
always been a rich source
of artistic inspiration. The
graceful sailing vessel of the
nineteenth century proved
to be an especially popular
image, as these lovely
snuff boxes show.

BELOW RIGHT
ENGRAVED
SPERM WHALE TOOTH,
CIRCA 1840
Unknown artist
Length 7 ½"
Though usually untrained
as artists, whalemen
recorded the technical
aspects of whale fishery
with accuracy. This large
example is one of at least
three nearly identical teeth
fashioned by the same hand.

RIGHT
STAFFORDSHIRE CHINA FIGURE,
CIRCA 1850
Unknown maker
Height 16 ¾"
In this sentimental grouping,
a sailor carries a toy yacht
while the small child at his
side begs for alms. The lot
of many seamen in the
nineteenth century was
difficult due to low wages
and often spendthrift habits.
Gift of Mrs. Charles
Bispham Levey

ABOVE
TATTOO MAN FIGURE,
EARLY TWENTIETH CENTURY
Unknown maker
Height 20 ¾"
The art of tattooing was
introduced to the West
following Cook's first voyage
to the Pacific in the 1760s,
and by the nineteenth century
tattoo parlors had sprung up
in ports around the world.
This figure stood in the
window of A.B. "Bill"
Coleman's famous tattoo
parlor in Norfolk, Virginia.

ABOVE
SAILOR'S VALENTINE SHELLWORK,
CIRCA 1870
Unknown maker
Width 20"
In the West Indies during the
latter nineteenth century,
"sailor's valentines"—intri-
cate, colorful shell arrange-
ments usually cased in
octagonal wooden boxes—
became a popular trinket for
Jack Tar. Many of these pieces
became treasured keepsakes
for loved ones back home.

ABOVE
LUSTERWARE BOWL
COMMEMORATING
GREAT EASTERN, CIRCA 1860
Scott Brothers &
Company, maker
Diameter 11 ¾"
Maritime events like the
launch of the steamship *Great
Eastern* in 1858 were well
chronicled by the potters
of England. For forty years
the 22,500-ton steamer was
the largest vessel built, and
came to symbolize Britain's
maritime supremacy.

RIGHT
ENGRAVED SPERM
WHALE TOOTH,
CIRCA 1875
Unknown artist
Height 8 ¼"
Large teeth like this one
served as ivory "canvases"
upon which an endless
variety of imagery was
engraved or carved. In
this instance, the whaleman
traced portraits of fash-
ionably dressed women
from a magazine illustration.

MODEL OF VENETIAN GALLEASS,
TWENTIETH CENTURY
August F. Crabtree,
modelmaker
Scale 1:48; length 44 ¼"
The galleass was a hybrid
of the multi-oared galley and
the pure oceangoing sailing
vessel. Whether sailed or
rowed, the vessel was an
impressive sight indeed. This
elaborate model, amazing
even by Crabtree standards,
represents a Venetian craft
of the mid-1600s.

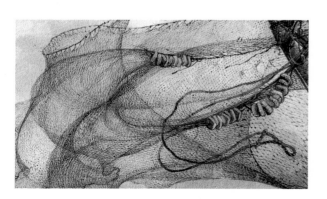

ABOVE AND DETAILS
(TOP AND BOTTOM)
*VIOLENT SQUALL ON
THE ADRIATIC*, 1856
Edward William Cooke
(English, 1811-1880)
Oil on canvas, 42" x 68"
Like so many of his
contemporaries, Cooke
developed an enduring
fascination with Venice.
At the center of the painting
a *bragozzo*, a traditional
sailing barge of the northern
Adriatic, races for safety as
a squall nips at her heels.

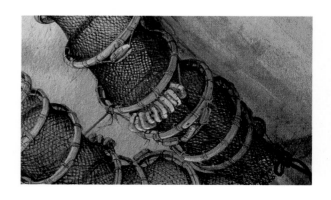

TOWBOAT AMERICA, 1853
James Bard
(American, 1815-1897)
Oil on canvas, 34" x 53"
During the nineteenth century, the task of moving huge amounts of cargo along the Hudson fell to specialized towboats like the *America*. James Bard, together with his twin brother, John, documented this vital period of American commerce through precise, highly detailed portraits like this.

HERRING DIPPER, CIRCA 1912
Philip Little
(American, 1857-1942)
Oil on canvas, 50" x 40"
By the time Little began painting, the Impressionist movement had taken hold in this country. His portrait of a doryman netting herring contains little exacting detail, but emphasizes the shimmering interplay of light, water, and iridescent fish scales.

THE WRECK OF THE HALSEWELL, CIRCA 1786
George Morland
(English, 1763-1804)
Oil on linen, 34"x 44 ¼"
Most of the *Halsewell*'s crew and passengers, including Captain Richard Pierce and his two daughters, were killed when the ship was driven onto the rocks off the Dorset coast in 1786. The popularity of paintings like this attests to the public's fascination with the tragedy.

LEFT
FIGUREHEAD OF A LADY WITH A
ROSE, CIRCA 1795-1815
Unknown carver
Height 35 ½"
The figure's high-waisted,
square-necked gown sug-
gests that she was carved
during the early nineteenth
century. She may have been
carried on the ship *Rose in
Bloom*, built in 1810 in
Connecticut.

OPPOSITE PAGE, BELOW
FIGUREHEAD OF AN INDIAN, FIRST
HALF OF NINETEENTH CENTURY
Unknown carver
Height 42"
Since the sixteenth century,
European artists had used
images of Native Americans to
symbolize the fecundity and
unspoiled quality of the New
World. This figurehead
probably graced the prow of
an English vessel engaged in
East Indian trade.

BELOW
PADDLEBOX ORNAMENT,
CIRCA 1867
Unknown carver
Height 31 ½"
As figureheads disappeared
from steamboats' increasingly
steep stems, carvers turned
their attention to other decor-
ations such as paddlebox
ornaments. This carving,
based on the Massachusetts
state seal, was probably
carried on the 1867 sidewheel
steamboat *Cambridge*.

LEFT
FIGUREHEAD FROM
EDMONTON, 1882
Attributed to John Rogerson
(Scots-Canadian, 1837-1925)
Height 91"
The 1,297-ton bark *Edmonton*,
built near Quebec in 1882,
carried this figurehead for
fourteen years. The *London
Shipping Journal* described
Rogerson, the probable carver,
as "the best workman on the
other side of the Atlantic."

RIGHT
FIGUREHEAD FROM BARKENTINE
BEAR OF OAKLAND, CIRCA 1874
Unknown carver
Height 57 ¼"
This polar bear figurehead
was an emblem of the ship's
destination and function:
Arctic seal hunting. Following
his celebrated Antarctic ex-
pedition, Admiral Richard E.
Byrd presented the figurehead
to The Mariners' Museum. Gift
of Admiral Richard E. Byrd

Paths of Commerce

The profound influence of sea commerce upon the wealth and strength of countries was clearly seen long before the true principles which governed its growth and prosperity were detected.

– CAPTAIN ALFRED THAYER MAHAN, USN, *The Influence of Sea Power Upon History, 1660-1783*, 1890

Historically, humans have sought the path of least resistance in establishing routes of trade and communication. In their quests to extend commercial and political influence over the oceans, cultures and empires around the globe have contributed greatly to our knowledge of the world. Data on winds and currents gathered in this process have proved particularly valuable in the establishment of sea routes.

The exchange of goods and ideas so central to the concept of commerce has driven nations to extend what Mahan termed "lines of travel" to all parts of the globe. Over the centuries great wealth has been spent improving navigational and safety aids and maintaining naval forces to protect or interdict the vessels that ply the world's waters. Today more than 90 percent of raw or manufactured items still travel by sea.

Commerce also includes such activities as fishing, which has historically provided not only food but, in Europe and America in particular, a training ground for merchant mariners. The harvesting of sea resources such as oil, gas, and manganese can also be called commerce. Water recreation constitutes commerce in another form and is one of the fastest-growing types of maritime activity.

ABOVE (DETAIL) AND BELOW
BONITO CANOE, 1939
Henry Kuper, builder
Length 20'
Canoes like this example
from the lower Solomon
Islands were used for
celebrating the *malaohu*, a
rite of passage for the sons
of island village chieftains.
Less ornate canoes were
used to catch bonito, a
tuna-like fish.

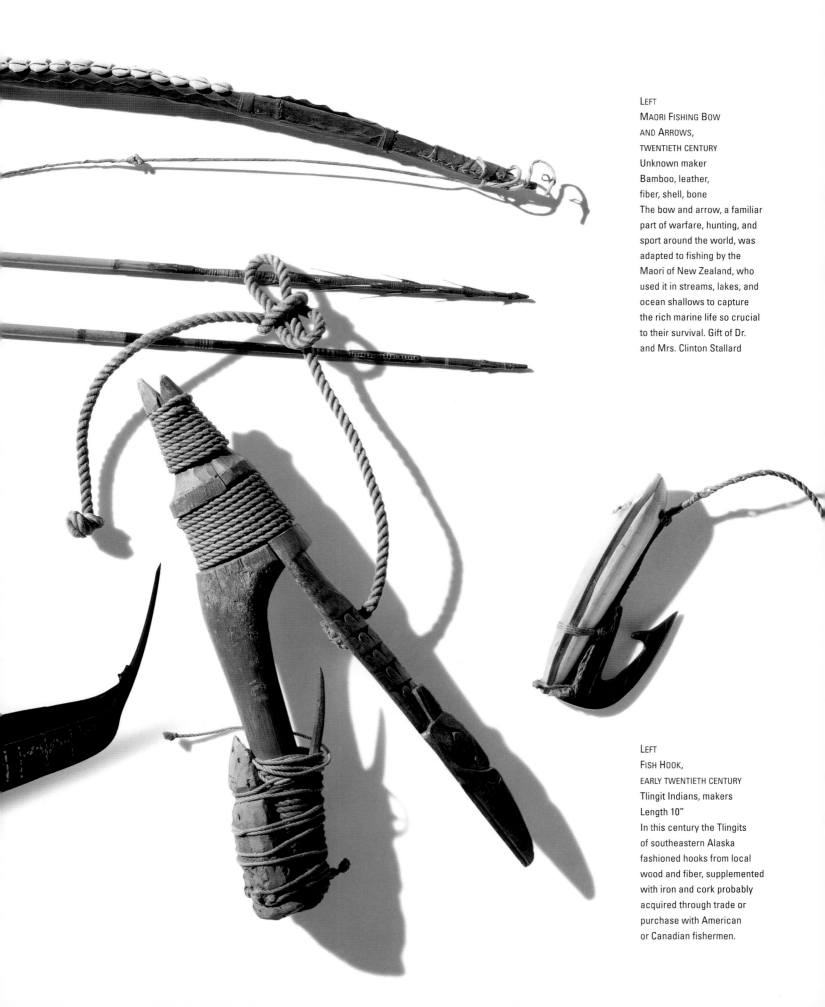

LEFT
**MAORI FISHING BOW
AND ARROWS,**
TWENTIETH CENTURY
Unknown maker
Bamboo, leather,
fiber, shell, bone
The bow and arrow, a familiar
part of warfare, hunting, and
sport around the world, was
adapted to fishing by the
Maori of New Zealand, who
used it in streams, lakes, and
ocean shallows to capture
the rich marine life so crucial
to their survival. Gift of Dr.
and Mrs. Clinton Stallard

LEFT
FISH HOOK,
EARLY TWENTIETH CENTURY
Tlingit Indians, makers
Length 10"
In this century the Tlingits
of southeastern Alaska
fashioned hooks from local
wood and fiber, supplemented
with iron and cork probably
acquired through trade or
purchase with American
or Canadian fishermen.

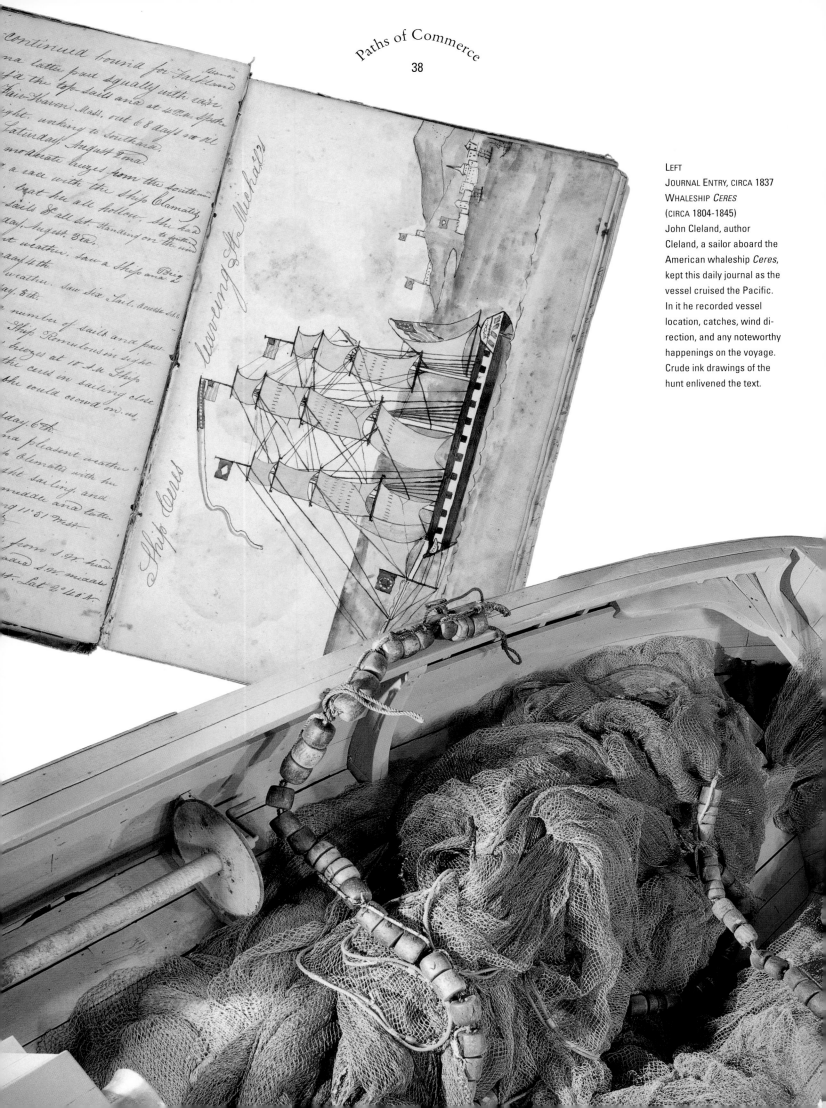

BELOW
POWERED MENHADEN PURSE
SEINE BOAT, CIRCA 1935
Barber Boatworks or
Cannon Boatworks, builders
Length 33'10"
From the American menhaden
fishery evolved several distinct
types of craft, among them the
purse seine boat. Operating in
pairs from a mother ship, these
ruggedly-built craft deployed
a large seine net for encircling
a school of menhaden. Gift
of the Standard Products
Company, Inc.

RIGHT
CHESAPEAKE BAY DEADRISE
WORKBOAT *MARINER*, 1980
Billy Moore, builder
Length 30'
Mariner, crafted by a skilled
local boatbuilder, was
designed primarily to harvest
oysters on the waters of the
Chesapeake Bay. The boat
combines modern
technology with traditional
techniques honed over nearly
a century. *Mariner*'s construction was carefully
documented to ensure that
an understanding of this
long-evolving local tradition
will survive. Constructed
for The Mariners' Museum
and the National Trust for
Historic Preservation

ABOVE
MODEL OF LIFEBOAT
MAUDE HARGREAVES,
CIRCA 1880
Unknown modelmaker
Scale 1:20; length 20 ¾"
Beginning in the nineteenth
century, sophisticated
coastal lifeboats were
developed and deployed
along Britain's treacherous
shores. So successful were
self-righting lifeboats like the
Maude Hargreaves that they
were quickly adopted by the
U.S. Lifesaving Service.

BELOW
MODEL OF NEW YORK CITY
FIREBOAT *FIRE FIGHTER*, 1990
Greg McKay, modelmaker
Scale 1:48; length 34 ½"
Fireboats were developed
to battle waterfront blazes
and shipboard fires. Designed
by Gibbs & Cox, *Fire Fighter*
was the world's most powerful fireboat when delivered
in 1938.

RIGHT
MODEL OF *LIGHTSHIP NO. 40*,
1876
James C. Wignall,
modelmaker
Scale 1:16; length 7'9 ¼"
Lightships—floating
lighthouses serving offshore
stations—were part of the
government's overall maritime
navigation system. *Lightship
No. 40*, built in 1875 for the
U.S. Lighthouse Board and
equipped with a steam-
powered fog signal, served
off the Massachusetts and
Delaware coasts. Gift of
the U.S. Coast Guard

ABOVE
MODEL OF FRENCH COASTAL
LIFEBOAT AND CARRIAGE, 1896
Eugene Cossec, modelmaker
Scale 1:25; length 15 ¾"
Launched from a special
beach carriage, this lifeboat
would be rowed through
the surf toward the wrecked
vessel. The maker of this
model was in charge of
a French lifesaving station
on the coast of Brittany
near St. Nazaire. Gift of
Miss Suzanne Wilkinson

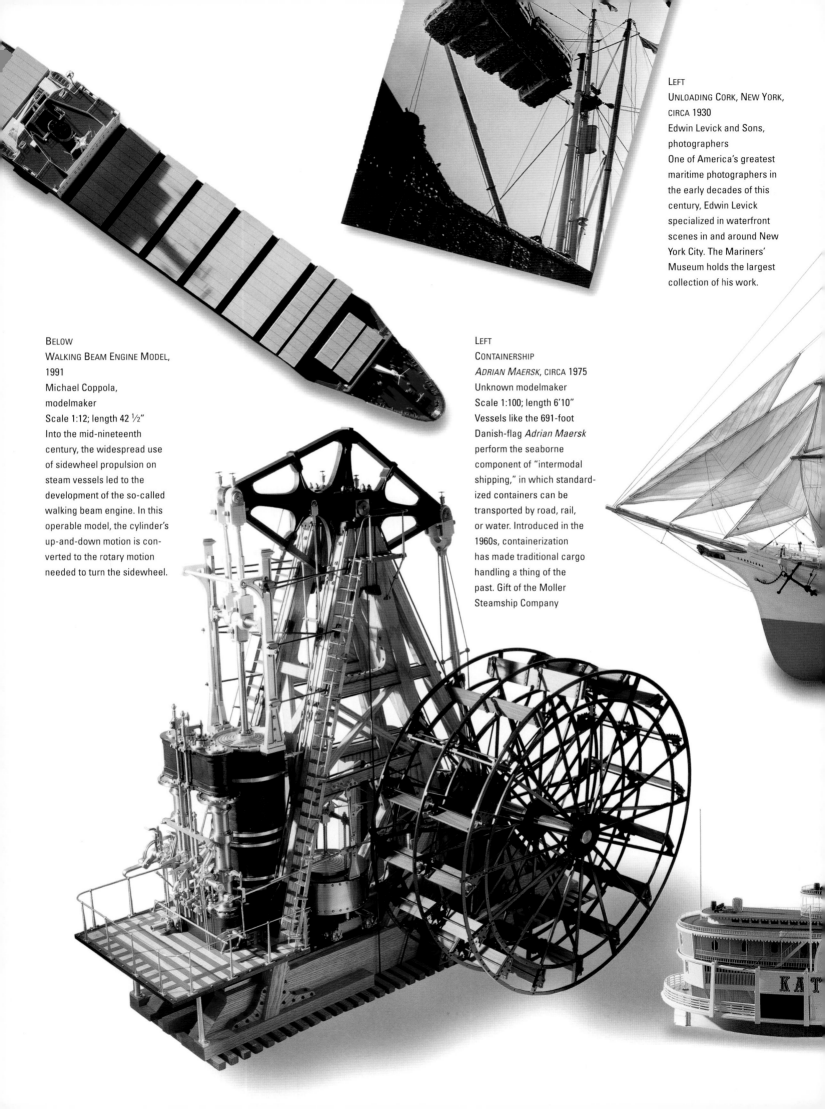

LEFT

UNLOADING CORK, NEW YORK, CIRCA 1930
Edwin Levick and Sons, photographers
One of America's greatest maritime photographers in the early decades of this century, Edwin Levick specialized in waterfront scenes in and around New York City. The Mariners' Museum holds the largest collection of his work.

BELOW

WALKING BEAM ENGINE MODEL, 1991
Michael Coppola, modelmaker
Scale 1:12; length 42 ½"
Into the mid-nineteenth century, the widespread use of sidewheel propulsion on steam vessels led to the development of the so-called walking beam engine. In this operable model, the cylinder's up-and-down motion is converted to the rotary motion needed to turn the sidewheel.

LEFT

CONTAINERSHIP
ADRIAN MAERSK, CIRCA 1975
Unknown modelmaker
Scale 1:100; length 6'10"
Vessels like the 691-foot Danish-flag Adrian Maersk perform the seaborne component of "intermodal shipping," in which standardized containers can be transported by road, rail, or water. Introduced in the 1960s, containerization has made traditional cargo handling a thing of the past. Gift of the Moller Steamship Company

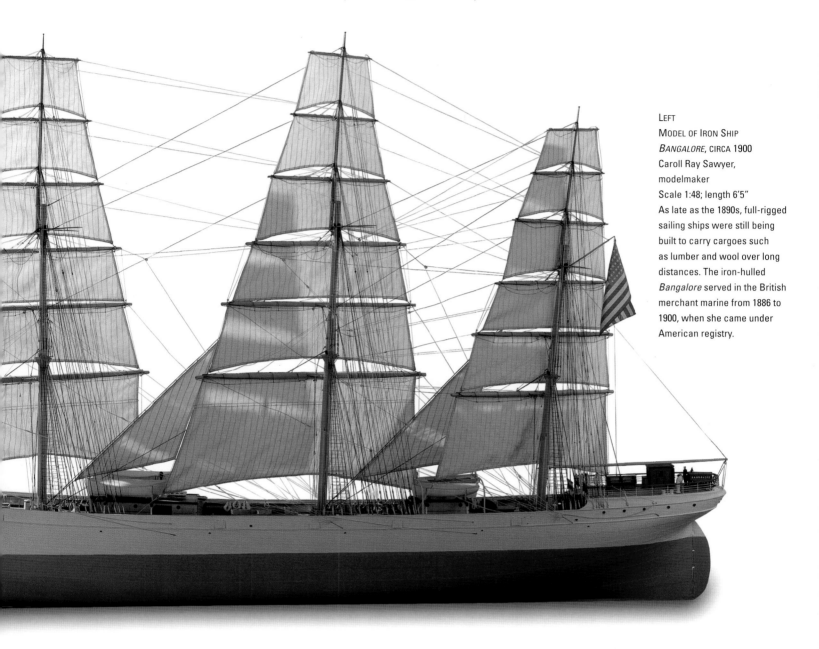

LEFT

MODEL OF IRON SHIP
BANGALORE, CIRCA 1900
Caroll Ray Sawyer,
modelmaker
Scale 1:48; length 6'5"
As late as the 1890s, full-rigged
sailing ships were still being
built to carry cargoes such
as lumber and wool over long
distances. The iron-hulled
Bangalore served in the British
merchant marine from 1886 to
1900, when she came under
American registry.

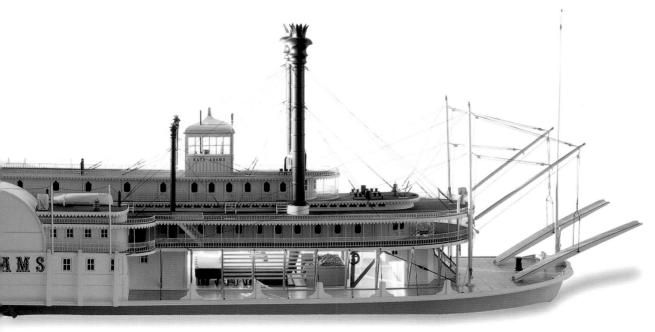

LEFT

MODEL OF STEAMBOAT
KATE ADAMS, CIRCA 1976
Robert G.C. Fee,
Marvin L. Bryant, and
Paris Aiken, modelmakers
Scale 1:48; length 5'7"
Built in 1882 for Mississippi
River mail packet service,
the 250-foot *Kate Adams*
was among the most lavishly
appointed river steamboats
in existence when she burned
in 1886. This superb model
shows the power and grace
of the American sidewheel
river steamboat in its heyday.

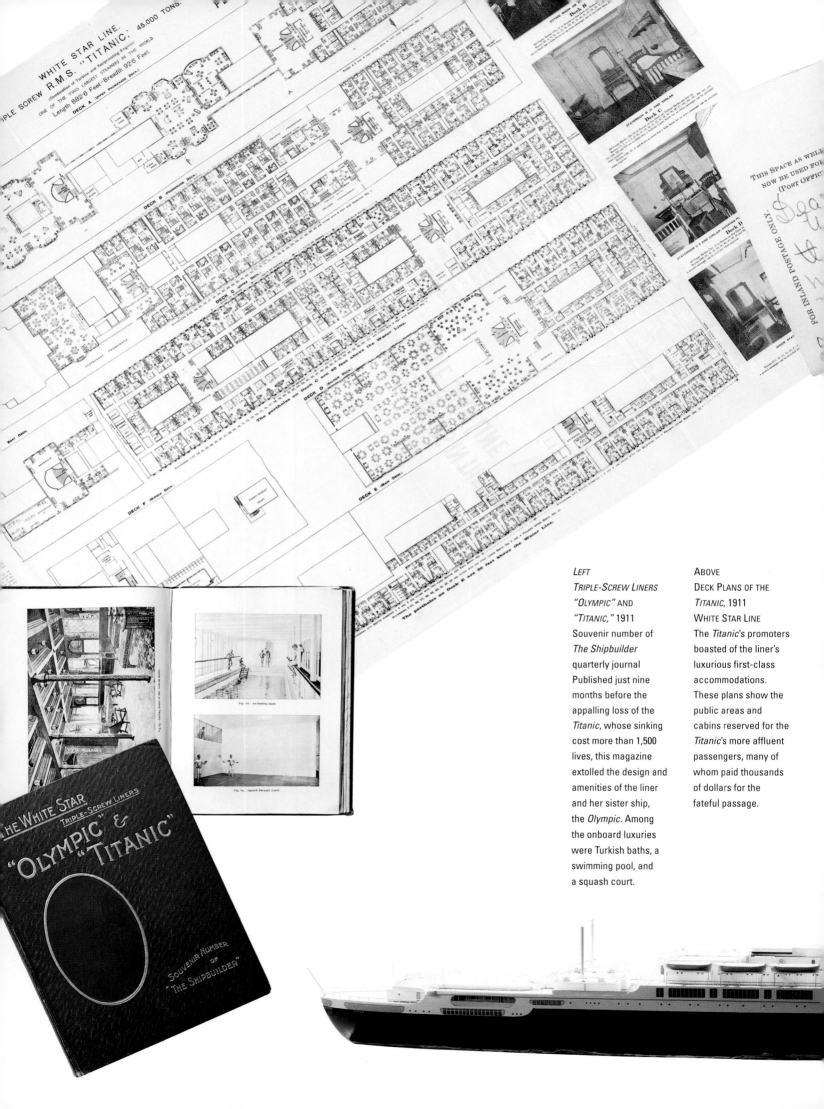

WHITE STAR LINE.
R.M.S. "TITANIC." 45,000 TONS.
TRIPLE SCREW (Combination of Turbine and Reciprocating Engines)
ONE OF THE TWO LARGEST STEAMERS IN THE WORLD
Length 852·6 Feet—Breadth 92·6 Feet.

DECK A (UPPER PROMENADE DECK.)

DECK B (PROMENADE DECK.)

DECK C (UPPER DECK.)

DECK D (SALOON DECK.)

The portholes on Deck C are 40 feet above the Water Line.

DECK E (MAIN DECK.)

DECK F (MIDDLE DECK.)

The portholes on Deck D are 30 feet above the Water Line.

The portholes on Deck E are 20 feet above the Water Line.

THIS SPACE AS WELL
NOW BE USED FOR
(POST OFFICE

FOR INLAND POSTAGE ONLY.

Fig. 28.—Swimming Bath.

Fig. 29.—Squash Racquet Court.

THE WHITE STAR
TRIPLE-SCREW LINERS
"OLYMPIC" &
"TITANIC"

SOUVENIR NUMBER
OF
"THE SHIPBUILDER"

LEFT
TRIPLE-SCREW LINERS
"OLYMPIC" AND
"TITANIC," 1911
Souvenir number of
The Shipbuilder
quarterly journal
Published just nine
months before the
appalling loss of the
Titanic, whose sinking
cost more than 1,500
lives, this magazine
extolled the design and
amenities of the liner
and her sister ship,
the *Olympic*. Among
the onboard luxuries
were Turkish baths, a
swimming pool, and
a squash court.

ABOVE
DECK PLANS OF THE
TITANIC, 1911
WHITE STAR LINE
The *Titanic*'s promoters
boasted of the liner's
luxurious first-class
accommodations.
These plans show the
public areas and
cabins reserved for the
Titanic's more affluent
passengers, many of
whom paid thousands
of dollars for the
fateful passage.

ABOVE
SILK POSTCARD FROM
RMS *CANOPIC*, 1910
The collection in The
Mariners' Museum
Research Library and
Archives includes
thousands of postcards
like the one shown here.
The RMS *Canopic* was
built in 1900 for the
White Star Line.

RIGHT
STAINED GLASS SKYLIGHT
FROM STEAMER *CITY OF
NORFOLK*, 1911
Unknown maker
Diameter 68"
Competing steamboat
companies equipped
their passenger vessels
with lavish amenities.
This remarkable skylight
dome graced the main
public area aboard the
Old Bay Line's steamer
City of Norfolk.

BELOW
MODEL OF
SS *UNITED STATES*,
CIRCA 1952
Gibbs & Cox, Inc.,
modelmaker
Scale 1:192;
length 62 1/16"
The superliner *United
States* was designed
by Gibbs & Cox, Inc.,
and built at Newport
News, Virginia, in 1951.
Crossing the Atlantic
in three and one-half
days on her maiden
voyage, the 53,000-ton
liner easily swept
aside the old speed
record. Gift of Gibbs
& Cox, Inc.

RIGHT
SS *UNITED STATES* MAKES
A CLEAN SWEEP ON
OFFICIAL TRIALS, 1952
Newport News
Shipbuilding
photograph
In an old maritime
tradition, a broom
signifying a "clean
sweep" was tied to the
masthead of the SS
United States as she
returned to Newport
News from her sea trials.
Gift of Newport News
Shipbuilding

ABOVE
MERCURY OUTBOARD MOTOR,
CIRCA 1988
Mercury Marine, maker
Length 64"
The revolutionary gasoline
outboards of the 1910s and
1920s have given way to high-
horsepower engines like this
six-cylinder, 115-h.p. model.

ABOVE
CHRIS-CRAFT RUNABOUT
MISS BELLE ISLE, 1923
Chris-Craft Corporation, builder
Length 26'
One of the oldest surviving
Chris-Crafts known, *Miss Belle
Isle* is a double-cockpit, ten-
passenger runabout whose
fine lines and elegant finish
bespeak a period of unbound-
ed optimism. Chris-Craft used
a modified Curtiss 8-cylinder
aircraft engine to propel
this boat.

RIGHT
AMERICA'S CUP PHOTOGRAPHS
VARIOUS PHOTOGRAPHERS
Originally known as the
"Hundred Guinea Cup,"
the trophy now called
the America's Cup was
presented in 1851 to the
New York Yacht Club's
America, which defeated
a fleet of fifteen British
yachts. The competition
is now the world's premier
yachting event.

LEFT
EVINRUDE 3 ½-H.P. OUTBOARD MOTOR, 1915
Evinrude Outboard Motor Company, maker
Length 34"
A mechanical genius, engineer Ole Evinrude designed and built his first outboard motor in the early 1900s. By 1909 he was producing a two-cycle, 1 ½-h.p. motor whose basic design would remain a standard for decades. Gift of Evinrude Motors, Division of OMC

ABOVE
CUTTER YACHT *VOLUNTEER*, 1887
Antonio Jacobsen
(Danish-American, 1815-1921)
Oil on canvas, 10 ¼" x 16"
With the America's Cup well established as the world's premier yachting event, the Americans fielded *Volunteer* in 1887, handily defeating the challenger *Thistle*. Antonio Jacobsen, best known for painting merchant steamships, also produced some very lively yachting views like this one.

BELOW
TUCKUP CATBOAT
THOMAS M. SEEDS, CIRCA 1875
James C. Wignall, builder
Length 14'9"
Developed as a workboat on the Delaware River, the tuckup catboat soon demonstrated its adeptness as a racer. A magazine article of the time noted that "Cowards and lazy men never sail in tuck-ups." Gift of Marion V. Brewington

Art and Science of Shipbuilding

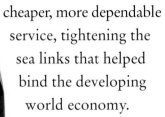

From the fashioning of the earliest wood raft or dugout, the shipbuilder has always had to look to the water for guidance, basing design and construction decisions on the features of the particular locale and the intended functions of the vessel.

For most of recorded history, wood was the chosen material, and a wide range of woodworking tools were developed for the construction of various craft. Knowledge and skills were passed from father to son and from master to apprentice in a form of oral history that continued into the nineteenth century. This tradition continues today in the case of certain regional small craft like the Chesapeake Bay deadrise boat.

With the Industrial Revolution came not only the use of iron and steel, but the introduction of steam for propulsion. Once freed of the whims of wind and tide, steam-powered ships could provide cheaper, more dependable service, tightening the sea links that helped bind the developing world economy.

The twentieth century has seen a great leap in the science of shipbuilding. Previously handed down from generation to generation, construction techniques now are guided by published data drawn from scientific study and experimentation. Computer-assisted design programs and sophisticated new tools aid the swift fabrication of vessels in steel and other materials.

The scope of wartime shipbuilding in this century, backed by a mobilized industrial economy, has dwarfed any previous effort. The scale of vessels, too, has increased to keep pace with a peacetime global economy in which manufacturer and consumer are often oceans apart.

RIGHT
SMOOTHING PLANE,
CIRCA 1680
Austrian
Colonial shipbuilders used planes to make special finished cuts and to smooth faces of planking. This example has a decorative ivory figure wearing a turban.

BELOW RIGHT
WILLIAM FRANCIS GIBBS
DRAFTING GEAR
Various makers
The relative simplicity of the tools used by naval architect William Francis Gibbs belies the complexity of designing modern merchant and naval vessels. Emphasizing speed, capacity, and survivability in the conceptual stage, Gibbs designed some of the most successful vessels of the era. Gift of Gibbs and Cox, Inc.

RIGHT
USS *FORRESTAL* UNDER CONSTRUCTION, 1955
Unknown photographer
Built at Newport News Shipbuilding and Dry Dock Company, the *Forrestal* was the first of a class of aircraft carriers that dwarfed even the enormous *Midway*, commissioned in 1945. The *Forrestal* was the first carrier designed with an angled flight deck to accommodate jet aircraft.

RIGHT
COLONIAL SHIPYARD DIORAMA,
1968-1973
Harold M. Hahn, modelmaker
Scale 1:96;
46 ⅝" x 27 ³/₁₆" x 27 ⅞"
In the eighteenth century
the availability of timber,
shipbuilding sites, and cheap
labor made American-built
vessels attractive, especially
for the growing trade between
England, North America, and
the West Indies. This diorama
shows American schooners
being built in the 1760s.

LEFT
CAULKING MALLET,
EIGHTEENTH CENTURY
Length 16 ½"
Caulking mallets like this
one were used for driving
fibrous materials like oakum
into vessel plank seams,
and were commonly found
in European and American
shipyards. Gift of Malcolm
Deschaux

LEFT
DIVIDERS, SEVENTEENTH
CENTURY
Length 22 ¼"
An important tool in
wooden ship and
boatbuilding, dividers
were used for transferring
dimensions onto timber.

BELOW
TIMBER MERCHANT'S GUIDE,
1823
Peter Guillet, author
Builders of wooden vessels
knew that curved components
were stronger if cut from
timber whose grain ran
with the shape of the part.
This small book offered
information on ways to use
various cuts from a tree.

Pl. 17.

Knee

Cable bitt

Cable bitt
Knee

Dimensions.

Smallest Size.		Largest Size.	
length	square	length	square
Feet	Inches	Feet	Inches
14	16 by 16	15	18 by 18
12	12 ~ 14	16	14 ~ 18

Lithographer

DRAWKNIFE,
MID-NINETEENTH CENTURY
BROAD AX, CIRCA 1890
MALLET, CIRCA 1890
Many basic wooden
boatbuilding tools such as
these have been in use for
centuries, and would have
been found in Chesapeake
Bay boatyards. Drawknife gift
of Mr. William D. Wilkinson

RIGHT
*NEW TABLE OF ALL THE
NAMES OF THE PRINCIPAL
PARTS AND RIGGING [OF] ...
A DUTCH MAN-OF-WAR,*
LATE SEVENTEENTH CENTURY
This drawing shows the
genius of Dutch ship design
and construction in the late
1600s. The flat bottoms,
reinforced interior con-
struction, and ornamental
stern designs shown here
were typical of Dutch naval
architecture of the period.

DRIVING DECK SPIKES,
PORTLAND SHIPBUILDING
COMPANY, PORTLAND, OREGON,
CIRCA 1918
Unknown photographer
The two shipyard workers in
the photograph are using
pneumatic hammers to drive
spikes in the wooden deck of
a vessel under construction.

RIVETING TOOLS
The rise of iron shipbuilding
in the nineteenth century
required workers trained
in new skills such as riveting.
Using tools like the air hammer,
hot cutter, passing tongs, and
backout punch, riveters fas-
tened metal plates, frames,
and beams together during
construction of the hull.

SAILMAKING TOOLS
Sailmaking traditionally took place in a sail loft—an open room or building large enough to accommodate the often bulky sails. Working on a long, low bench, the sailmaker used an array of special tools: sharp fids to pierce holes in the canvas, a heavy leather palm to push the needle through the material, and a seam rubber to flatten new seams and stitches.

RIGHT
SAILMAKER ALBERT BROWN, 1954
A. Aubrey Bodine, photographer
Bodine, a *Baltimore Sun* photographer, had a special feel for the beauty and distinct character of the Chesapeake Bay and the life of its watermen. Here he captures sailmaker Albert Brown in his sail loft on Deal's Island, Maryland.

WILLIAM FRANCIS GIBBS AND
THE SS *UNITED STATES*,
CIRCA 1952
Unknown photographer
Silver print, 8" x 10"
Naval architect William
Francis Gibbs (1886-1967)
was convinced that
vessels could be made
virtually fireproof. When
he designed the superliner
United States, it was said
that the only parts of the ship
that could burn were the
five grand pianos and the two
butcher's chopping blocks.
Courtesy of Frank Braynard

WILLIAM FRANCIS GIBBS'S
DRAFTING TABLE, CIRCA 1940
Sitting on a tall stool in his
office overlooking the Hudson
River, Gibbs directed the
activities of thousands of
employees. His firm, Gibbs
& Cox, Inc., produced 700
acres of blueprints annually
during World War II. Gift
of Frederic H. Gibbs

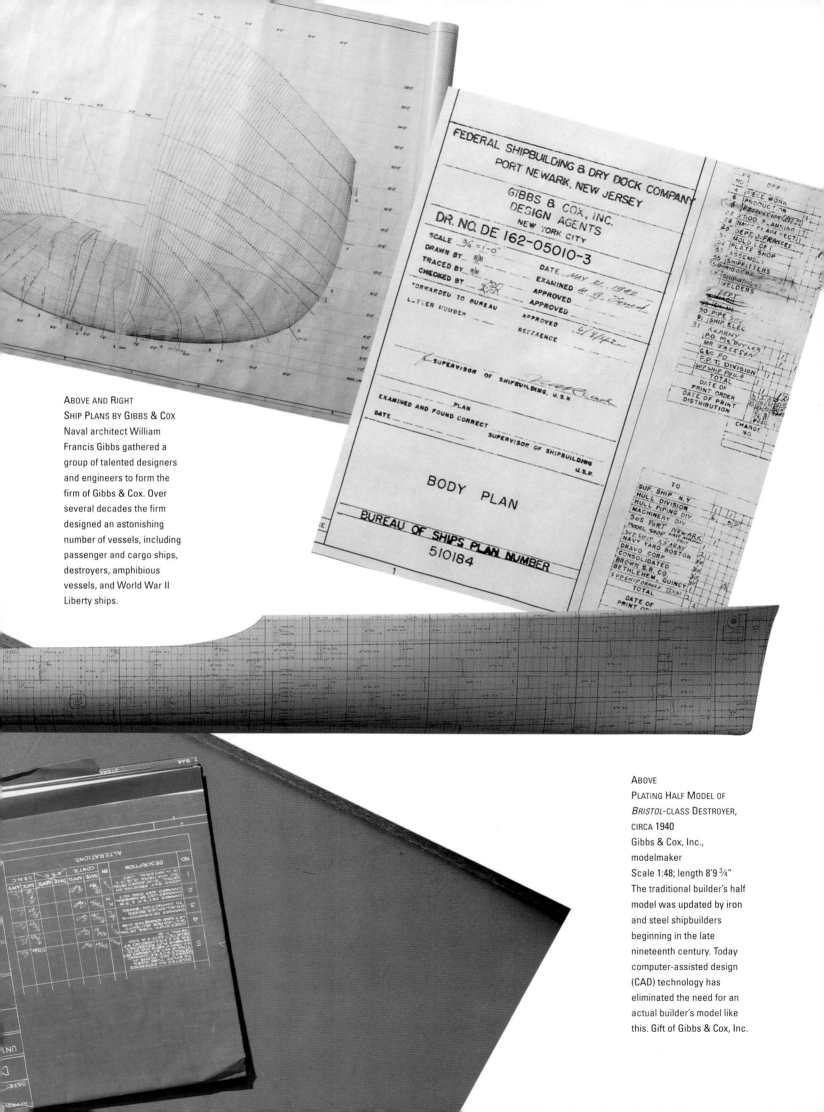

ABOVE AND RIGHT
SHIP PLANS BY GIBBS & COX
Naval architect William
Francis Gibbs gathered a
group of talented designers
and engineers to form the
firm of Gibbs & Cox. Over
several decades the firm
designed an astonishing
number of vessels, including
passenger and cargo ships,
destroyers, amphibious
vessels, and World War II
Liberty ships.

ABOVE
PLATING HALF MODEL OF
BRISTOL-CLASS DESTROYER,
CIRCA 1940
Gibbs & Cox, Inc.,
modelmaker
Scale 1:48; length 8'9 ¾"
The traditional builder's half
model was updated by iron
and steel shipbuilders
beginning in the late
nineteenth century. Today
computer-assisted design
(CAD) technology has
eliminated the need for an
actual builder's model like
this. Gift of Gibbs & Cox, Inc.

Commanding the Sea

Who-ever commands the sea, commands the trade, whoever commands the trade of the world, commands the riches of the world, and consequently the world itself.

– SIR WALTER RALEIGH (1552-1618)

Just as commerce has followed exploration and settlement, organized national navies have developed for the protection of that commerce. By the seventeenth century, the rise of transoceanic European empires prompted the birth of structured naval forces. Whether patrolling colonial stations or convoying merchant ships along established trade routes, these agents of national policy proved indispensable.

Born of the dominant maritime power of the age, the United States understood the need for a naval force to complement its growing merchant fleet. Through much of the U.S. Navy's first century, the emphasis was on diplomacy and the defense of coast and commerce.

In this century, advances in propulsion and communication, navigation and detection devices, even aircraft and submarines, have helped the nation project its influence across the sea. Through two world wars and other regional conflicts, the navy has proved crucial for protecting lines of supply or carrying the war to the enemy. The strategically placed warship has also played a role in diplomatic efforts to maintain peace. And peacetime applications of naval technology like satellite positioning systems have allowed the exploration of the seas by scientists, archaeologists, and historians, by whose work all of humankind gains.

RIGHT
MEDAL COMMEMORATING THE GREAT WHITE FLEET, 1907
Brass 3 ⅛" x 2 ⅜"
On December 16, 1907, the United States Atlantic Fleet, which came to be known as the Great White Fleet, departed Hampton Roads on a largely symbolic cruise around the world. The show of power helped establish the United States as a force to be reckoned with on the international scene.

BELOW
MODEL OF ICE BREAKER
USS *GLACIER*, CIRCA 1955
Ingalls Shipbuilding Corporation, modelmaker
Scale 1:96; length 38 ⅞"
Ensuring safe passage for vessels in ice-choked waters is the traditional task of ice breakers. Equipped with powerful diesel engines, *Glacier* had a distinctive bow designed to ride up over thick ice and use the vessel's own weight to break open a path.
Gift of Ingalls Shipbuilding Corporation

RIGHT
USS *CONNECTICUT*, 1907
Unknown photographer
The new battleship *Connecticut*, flagship of the Great White Fleet, led fifteen other battleships and auxiliary vessels on the famous 1907 cruise around the world. The voyage covered 46,000 miles and included stops at such strategic points as Amoy, China, and the Suez Canal.

RIGHT
ARBALEST,
POSSIBLY SEVENTEENTH CENTURY
Unknown maker
Length 47"
The introduction of accurate
and powerful bow-strung
weapons like the crossbow
had a profound effect on the
conduct of military—and
naval—engagements. This
arbalest, an improvement on
the crossbow, rapidly earned
the respect of combatants
afloat and ashore.

RIGHT
DOCKYARD MODEL OF FRENCH
96-GUN SHIP OF THE LINE, 1805
Unknown maker
Scale ⅓"=1'; length 80 ½"
Dockyard models were used
to communicate the details
of a vessel's construction
to governmental boards
unaccustomed to reading
architects' drawings. They
were rarely rigged, as rigging
was fairly standardized. This
example is thought to have
been a teaching model. Gift
of the Kriegstein Ship
Model Collection

RIGHT
BRONZE *LANTAKA*, LATE
SEVENTEENTH CENTURY
Unknown maker
Length 48"
The *lantaka*, a cast bronze
swivel gun developed in
the seventeenth century,
found use from the Medi-
terranean to the western
Pacific. This example is
attributed to Philippine
pirates circa 1700.

OPPOSITE PAGE
FRONTISPIECE FROM *ZEE-ATLAS
OFTE WATERWERELD*, 1683
Hendrik Doncker
(Dutch, seventeenth century)
Many important seventeenth-
century navigational works
were published in Amsterdam.
Among them were Doncker's
Zee-Atlas, first issued in 1659.
Such works were often trans-
lated into English, French,
and Spanish.

RIGHT
DESTRUCTION OF THE FRENCH
FLEET OFF THE NILE, ON THE 1ST
OF AUGUST, 1798 ...
Robert Cleveley
(English, 1747-1809)
Oil on canvas, 29 ⅛″ x 41 ½″
In this painting Cleveley, a
former ship-caulker and
seaman who was later
appointed Draughtsman to
His Royal Highness, doc-
uments the English navy's
defeat of the French fleet
in Aboukir Bay during the
Napoleonic Wars. The
victory ensured lasting
fame for Horatio Nelson,
who led the attack.

BELOW
TEA CADDY
Island Leadworks,
London, maker
Height 6 ½″
Nelson's glorious death at
Trafalgar set in motion a
commemorative industry that
thrives even today. The
medallions on this painted
lead box are typical of the
post-Trafalgar period.
Gift of James E. Jewell

RIGHT
ENGRAVING OF THE DEATH OF NELSON, 1873
Engraved by C.W. Sharpe; painted by D. Maclise R.A.
17 ½″ x 48 ½″
Nelson was aboard HMS *Victory* at Trafalgar in 1805 when
he was fatally wounded by a French sharpshooter. His
death triggered an unparalleled outpouring of national
grief in Britain and added a bittersweet quality to the
British victory over a combined Franco-Spanish fleet.
Gift of Lily Lambert McCarthy

ABOVE
ETCHED GLASS RUMMER,
IN MEMORY OF LORD NELSON
JANY 9 1806
Unknown maker
Height 7"
A flood of memorabilia followed Lord Nelson's death
at the Battle of Trafalgar.
His elaborate state funeral
was a favorite subject, as
shown in this footed drinking
glass or "rummer." No naval
hero has been so widely
commemorated in glass
or ceramics as Nelson.

ABOVE
FABRIC SAMPLER, 1801
Mary Onions Ann Rhead,
maker
14" x 15 ¼"
Nelson's naval achievements
inspired the children of
England as well as their
elders. Thirteen-year-old
Mary Rhead stitched this
sampler in 1801, the year in
which Nelson defeated the
Danish fleet at Copenhagen.
Gift of Mrs. John G. McCarthy

BELOW
LETTER FROM LORD ADMIRAL
HORATIO NELSON TO
SIR ALEXANDER BALL,
JULY 10, 1803
When he wrote this letter to
the British governor of Malta,
Nelson was en route to join
the British blockade against
Napoleon at Toulon. In it he
explains his intention of re-
lying heavily on the expertise
of Sir Richard Bickerton, his
second in command.

RIGHT
PICTURES OF PEOPLE ON BOARD A STEAMBOAT, 1853
Unknown Japanese artist
Woodcut, 13" x 18 ½"
The Perry expedition to Japan aimed to "open up" the insular nation to the economies of the west, in particular that of the United States. The participation of some of the most advanced warships of the period also served notice of American naval power. A Japanese artist recorded his impressions in this marvelous print series.

ABOVE
UNITED STATES NAVY POWDER FLASK, CIRCA 1840S
Copper
Height 9 ¾"
This heavy powder flask, used for priming cannons, held 14 ounces of powder and dispensed charges averaging 65 grams. Three different contractors made flasks of this type in the decades preceding the Civil War.

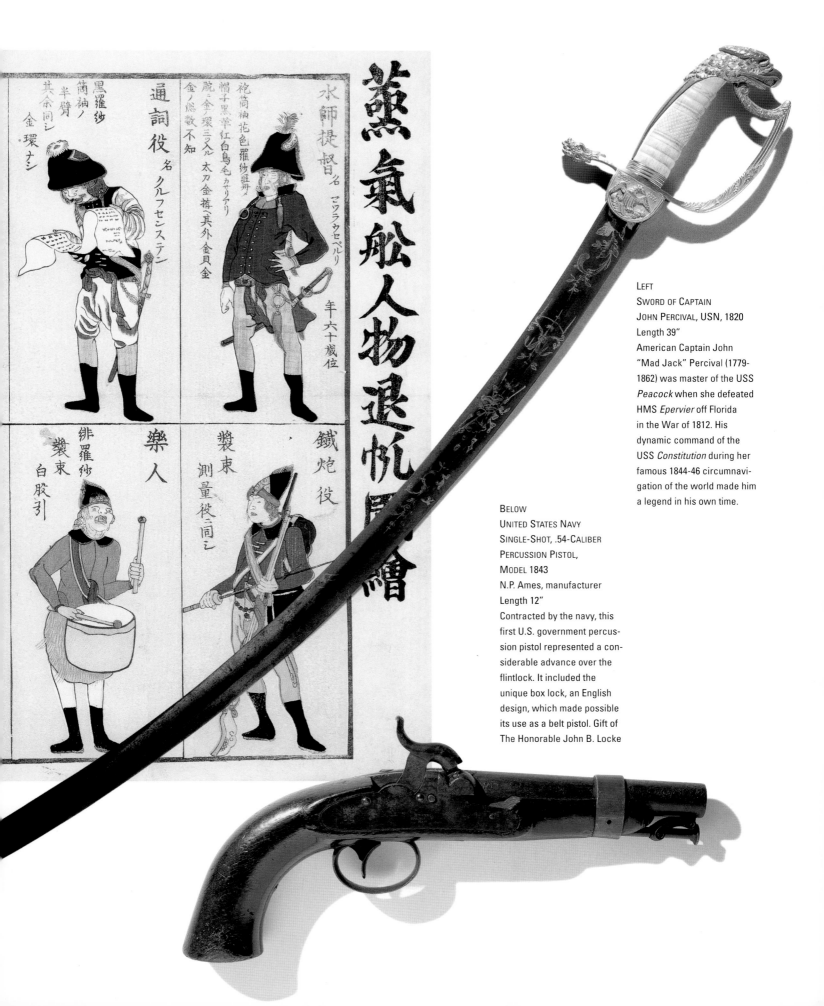

LEFT
SWORD OF CAPTAIN
JOHN PERCIVAL, USN, 1820
Length 39"
American Captain John
"Mad Jack" Percival (1779-
1862) was master of the USS
Peacock when she defeated
HMS *Epervier* off Florida
in the War of 1812. His
dynamic command of the
USS *Constitution* during her
famous 1844-46 circumnavi-
gation of the world made him
a legend in his own time.

BELOW
UNITED STATES NAVY
SINGLE-SHOT, .54-CALIBER
PERCUSSION PISTOL,
MODEL 1843
N.P. Ames, manufacturer
Length 12"
Contracted by the navy, this
first U.S. government percus-
sion pistol represented a con-
siderable advance over the
flintlock. It included the
unique box lock, an English
design, which made possible
its use as a belt pistol. Gift of
The Honorable John B. Locke

LEFT
ITEMS FROM THE ALBUM OF
LIEUTENANT J.P. WORDEN
Executive officer of the
Civil War ironclad USS
Monitor during her
momentous clash with
the CSS *Virginia*, Worden
later assembled this album
of *Monitor* memorabilia.
Shown here are scenes
of the crew and a later
portrait of Worden.

LEFT
MODEL OF THE
USS *MONITOR*, 1935
The Mariners' Museum
Model Shop, maker
Scale 1:48; length 43 ³⁄₈"
The *Monitor* made history
in March 1862 by engaging
the Confederate ironclad
Virginia in Hampton Roads
in the first combat between
ironclad vessels. John
Ericsson's shallow-draft,
low-profile design was
adopted by the Union Navy
for its new fleet of coastal
and river ironclads.

LEFT
ANCHOR OF THE
USS *MONITOR*, 1862
John Ericsson, designer
70" x 78" x 78"
This four-fluke, 1,350-pound
iron anchor, the only known
example of its type, was
recovered near the wreck
of the *Monitor* in 1983, one
hundred twenty-one years
after the famous Civil War
ironclad sank. Courtesy of
the National Oceanic and
Atmospheric Administration

ABOVE
MODEL OF THE
CSS *VIRGINIA*, 1936
The Mariners' Museum
Model Shop, maker
Scale 1:48; length 68 ³⁄₄"
The Confederate ironclad
Virginia was converted
from the steam frigate USS
Merrimack after it was
scuttled at Gosport Navy
Yard, Virginia. The huge
vessel sported a low,
sloping armored super-
structure and a reinforced
bow for ramming opponents.

RIGHT
STEERING WHEEL OF THE CSS
VIRGINIA, CIRCA 1856
Tredegar Iron Works,
Richmond, Virginia, maker
Diameter 56"
This iron wheel was originally
installed on the steam frigate
USS *Merrimack*. In April 1861
Union troops scuttled and
sank the *Merrimack* at the
Norfolk Navy Yard; six weeks
later the Confederates raised
the vessel, put her in dry
dock, and converted her into
the ironclad *Virginia*. Gift of
Tredegar Company

ABOVE
MODEL OF DESTROYER
USS *BAINBRIDGE*
R.G. Sketchley, modelmaker
Scale $^3/_{16}$" = 1'; length 58 $^9/_{16}$"
Completed and commissioned
in 1921, the four-stack
Bainbridge served in the
Mediterranean, the Atlantic,
and the Caribbean before
being assigned to the Pacific
Fleet. Decommissioned in
1937, she was recommissioned
in 1939 and served throughout
World War II. Gift of Mrs.
R.G. Sketchley

BELOW
FIRST FLIGHT FROM THE
DECK OF A SHIP, 1910
Kelville Glennen,
photographer
Flying a biplane from the
deck of the scout cruiser
Birmingham in Hampton
Roads in 1910, Eugene
Ely was the first to demon-
strate the possibilities of
aircraft at sea.

FOLLOW
THE
FLAG

LEFT
UNITED STATES NAVY
RECRUITMENT POSTER
"FOLLOW THE FLAG," 1917
J. Daugherty, Jr., artist
Color print, 28" x 42"
During World War I, the
U.S. government issued
hundreds of different posters
supporting a wide variety of
war aims. Twenty-five thou-
sand copies of this poster had
been issued by March 1918.

BELOW
MODEL OF FLEET SUBMARINE
USS REDFISH, 1959
Thomas J. Haynes,
modelmaker
Scale 1:48; length 6'6"
By 1942 a new breed of submarine was entering U.S.
Navy service. Known as
"fleet-type" subs, vessels
like the Redfish combined
long-range and heavy fire-
power and helped carry
out the war of attrition
against the Japanese.

ABOVE
AMPHIBIOUS OPERATIONS -
WORLD WAR II
Thomas C. Skinner
(American, 1888-1955)
Oil on canvas, 81" x 45"
Eleven landing ship docks
(LSDs) like the USS Comstock
were built at Newport News
during World War II to serve
both as mobile floating dry
docks for the repair of small
craft and as mother ships to
landing craft. The Comstock
was on her shakedown
cruise when the Japanese
surrendered in August 1945.

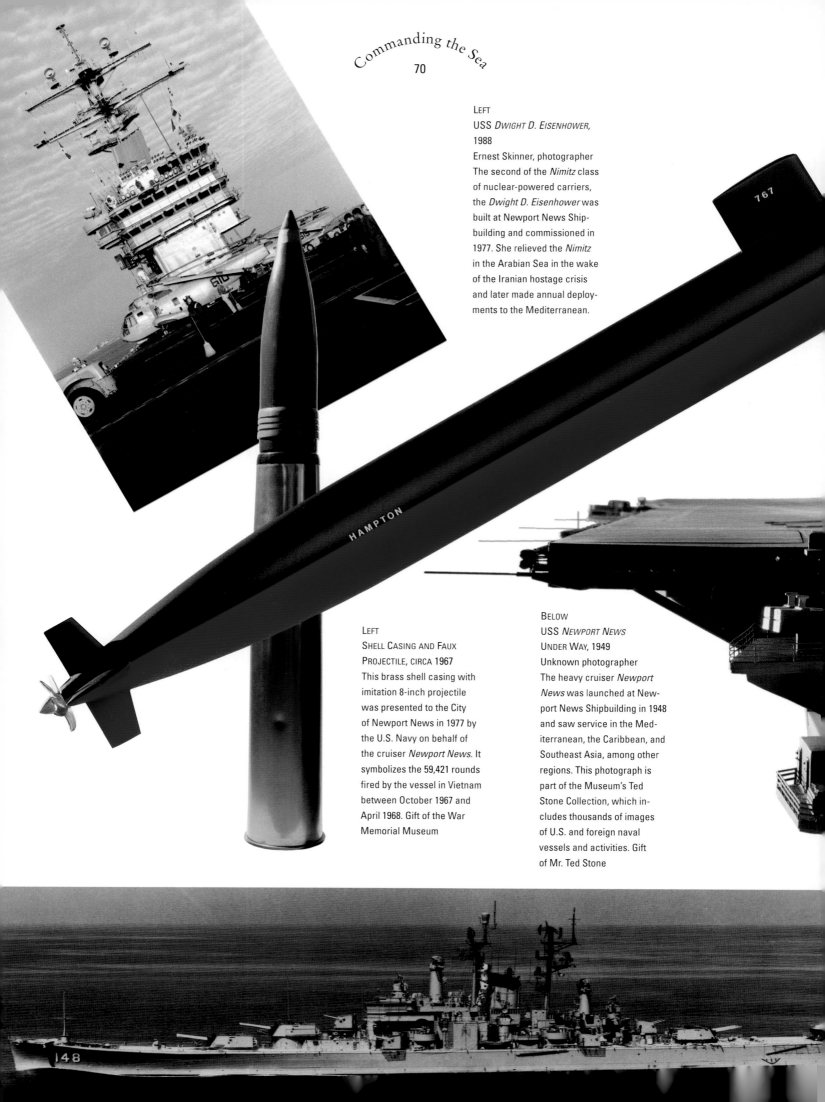

LEFT
USS *DWIGHT D. EISENHOWER*,
1988
Ernest Skinner, photographer
The second of the *Nimitz* class
of nuclear-powered carriers,
the *Dwight D. Eisenhower* was
built at Newport News Shipbuilding and commissioned in
1977. She relieved the *Nimitz*
in the Arabian Sea in the wake
of the Iranian hostage crisis
and later made annual deploy-
ments to the Mediterranean.

LEFT
SHELL CASING AND FAUX
PROJECTILE, CIRCA 1967
This brass shell casing with
imitation 8-inch projectile
was presented to the City
of Newport News in 1977 by
the U.S. Navy on behalf of
the cruiser *Newport News*. It
symbolizes the 59,421 rounds
fired by the vessel in Vietnam
between October 1967 and
April 1968. Gift of the War
Memorial Museum

BELOW
USS *NEWPORT NEWS*
UNDER WAY, 1949
Unknown photographer
The heavy cruiser *Newport
News* was launched at Newport News Shipbuilding in 1948
and saw service in the Mediterranean, the Caribbean, and
Southeast Asia, among other
regions. This photograph is
part of the Museum's Ted
Stone Collection, which includes thousands of images
of U.S. and foreign naval
vessels and activities. Gift
of Mr. Ted Stone

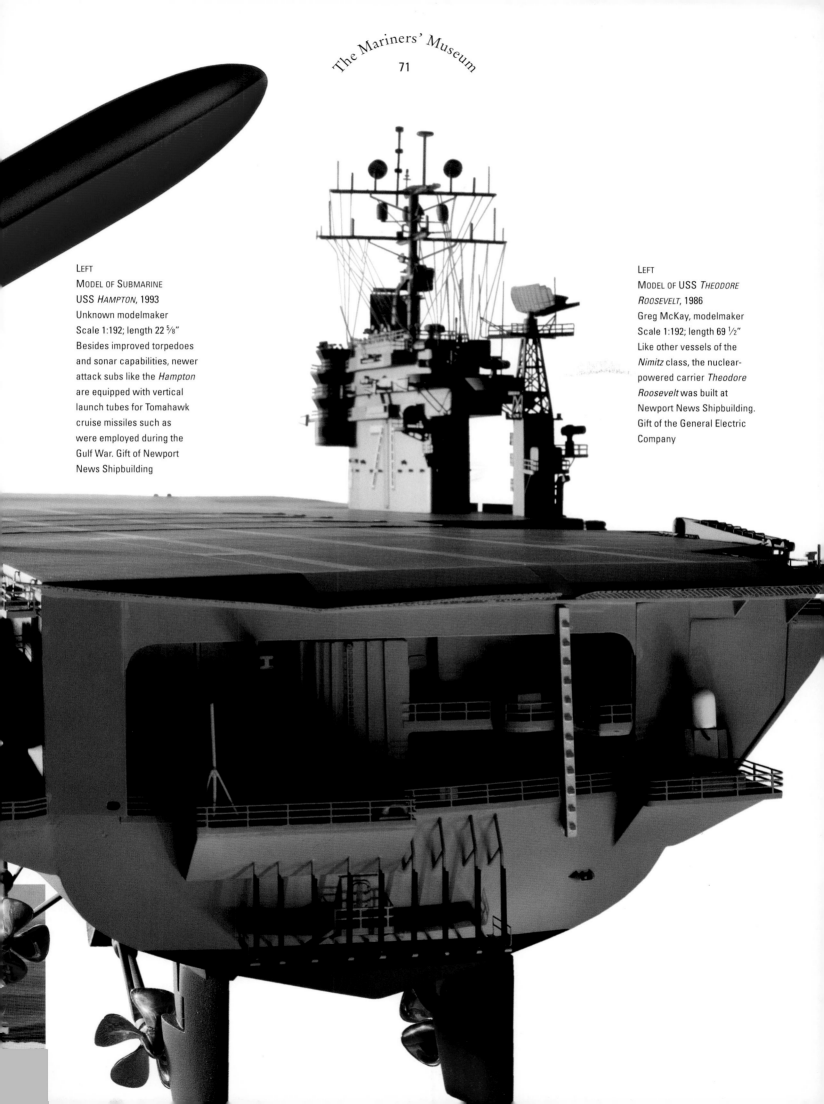

LEFT
MODEL OF SUBMARINE
USS *HAMPTON*, 1993
Unknown modelmaker
Scale 1:192; length 22 ⅝"
Besides improved torpedoes
and sonar capabilities, newer
attack subs like the *Hampton*
are equipped with vertical
launch tubes for Tomahawk
cruise missiles such as
were employed during the
Gulf War. Gift of Newport
News Shipbuilding

LEFT
MODEL OF USS *THEODORE
ROOSEVELT*, 1986
Greg McKay, modelmaker
Scale 1:192; length 69 ½"
Like other vessels of the
Nimitz class, the nuclear-
powered carrier *Theodore
Roosevelt* was built at
Newport News Shipbuilding.
Gift of the General Electric
Company